# Rex

Fulton Books
Meadville, PA

Published by Fulton Books 2024

ISBN 979-8-88982-206-6 (paperback)
ISBN 979-8-88982-207-3 (digital)

Printed in the United States of America

# Rex

## The Happiest Dog

## Stephanie Rouly

This is the true story about a dog named Rex and how he became a very loved member of the Rouly family.

One chilly day in December, Stephanie, mom of the family, was leaving for the grocery store. As she began to drive away from the house, she noticed a fluffy big dog walking on the sidewalk toward her. She stopped to see if he had a collar and identification tag, because it was a bit unusual to see a dog walking by itself. He had no collar and was clearly alone. Stephanie gave him a few pats on the head and watched him continue on his way up the street.

The next day, Stephanie was out watering flowers on the front porch when she spotted the dog walking by again. This time, Stephanie ran into the house to grab a bowl of water and some hot dogs for him. The family only had cats, so there was no dog food to give him. He happily ate his snack then continued on his way up the street.

Stephanie had told Chris, dad of the family, all about the beautiful fluffy brown dog that had been walking by the house each day. Chris was curious to meet him.

The next day, Stephanie and Chris were going Christmas shopping. As they were leaving the house, Stephanie spotted the dog walking up the street. It was a chilly and foggy morning, and the dog looked like a big bear walking through the mist. Chris was a little nervous about petting him!

Chris and Stephanie walked over to visit with him, and the dog was happy to have a new friend petting him. After a few pats from Chris, the dog continued on his way up the street.

While Chris and Stephanie were out shopping, they talked about what a nice dog he was and wondered if they should invite him to live with them. The family had two little girls that would surely like to have a pet dog. Chris and Stephanie bought some dog food while they were out so the dog would have proper food. When they came back from shopping, the dog was sitting in the driveway. The neighbor children said that the dog sat there all day, waiting for them to return.

The little girls, Hannah and Samantha, were very excited to have a new pet. What a wonderful early Christmas gift!

The Christmas Eve celebration was at the Rouly home, and all the relatives fell in love with the fluffy big brown dog. The Roulys decided to name him Rex.

10

Rex was a wonderful addition to the family. He loved playing fetch and had a favorite toy, a stuffed robot dog named Goddard. He also enjoyed spending time with his family. He would sit patiently while Samantha played tea party with him and her dolls.

13

He would cuddle up to Hannah on her bed if she were reading a book.

There would be silly time with Chris too. Chris would pat his chest and tell Rex, "Up." Rex would stand on his back legs and put his front paws on Chris' chest, and they would dance the cha-cha!

He really enjoyed going on car rides too! On Sunday mornings, Chris would go to the local doughnut shop and get treats for breakfast. Rex always rode along. He would sit in the back seat and look out the window like a person!

Although Rex usually had nice manners, sometimes he would take himself on his own walks. This usually happened when the girls came home from school in the afternoon. They would open the front door, and he would be waiting for them.

The minute it was opened just a crack, he would rush past them and run fast up the street. He would usually go visit with his dog friend, Willow. She was a tan little dog that looked like a deer. They would chase each other in the yard at Willow's house until they were both tired out.

21

A few times, he walked to the nearby grandparents' house. Granny and Papa would give him a few treats and some water and then drive him back home.

Rex loved his cat family too. Josie and Leo were his best friends. They would sit next to each other and cuddle. Sometimes Josie would pat his head and lick his ears.

When Rex was about five years old, he started having vision problems in one of his eyes. The veterinarian said that Rex had glaucoma and was going to go blind in that eye. The family read a lot of books about living with a blind dog and how to take care of him. Rex could still see well out of his other eye, but the Roulys wanted to be prepared. Rex learned new commands. When they told him "easy," it meant to slow down because something may be in the way. When he heard the word "up," he knew to step up at the curb. He was very smart and learned his new words quickly.

Rex was seven years old when his other eye developed glaucoma, and he was then totally blind. He was used to the commands of "easy" and "up," and being totally sightless wasn't too difficult for him. Dogs have wonderful cognitive abilities, and that memory helped him remember where the furniture was in the house and where the grass was in the backyard. He didn't bump into anything on accident too often and still enjoyed going on walks.

There are lots of interesting things to smell while you are on a walk outside. He was the same happy fluffy dog that he had always been.

26

He was so very loved and was the happiest dog. He was such a special part of the Rouly family for fourteen years before he took his walk over the Rainbow Bridge. He was one of a kind and will never be forgotten.

# About the Author

Stephanie Rouly is a Southern California native that loves animals (big and small), spending time with her family, reading, knitting, and traveling every chance she gets. Stephanie shares her Menifee home with husband, Chris, three cats, and one dog.

*Rex, The Happiest Dog* is Stephanie's first children's book.